mediation matters

Creating a peaceful school through peer mediation

Edward Sellman

Acknowledgements

I should like to express my gratitude to my colleague Belinda Harris for reviewing the original manuscript and to former colleagues, particularly from the West Midlands Quaker Peace Education Project, who have informed many of the ideas contained within this book.

Permission to photocopy
This book contains materials which may be reproduced by photocopier or other means for use by the purchaser. The permission is granted on the understanding that these copies will be used within the educational establishment of the purchaser. The book and all its contents remain copyright. Copies may be made without reference to the publisher or the licensing scheme for the making of photocopies operated by the Publishers' Licensing Agency.

The right of Edward Sellman to be identified as the author of this work has been asserted by him in accordance with sections 77 and 78 of the Copyright, Designs and Patents Act 1988.

Mediation Matters
100771
ISBN-13: 978 1 85503 472 3
© Edward Sellman
Cover illustration © Martin Sanders
Inside illustrations © Ray and Corinne Burrows
All rights reserved
First published 2008

Printed in the UK for LDA
Abbeygate House, East Road, Cambridge, CB1 1DB, UK

Key themes

Dovecote is an example of good practice, and no doubt it will continue to improve the scheme. The following key themes, extracted from the case study, serve to summarise many of the issues discussed within this book.

Whole-school approach

In the case study peer mediation is not an isolated service. It is integrated with many other aspects of the school culture. This is very important in ensuring conflict is managed in a consistent and peaceful manner throughout the entire school. The ideal vehicle for achieving consistency between the communication practices of teachers and the language of mediation is to supplement peer mediation training with quality staff training.

Staff support

The service enjoys the backing of the headteacher and the commitment of a dedicated service co-ordinator, school governor and local authority support team. These are essential ingredients for establishing a critical mass of support for the initiative. The principles of peer mediation should also inform the induction of new staff members to ensure this support is maintained.

Consistency between principles

Consistency between the principles of mediation and other school practices is an area of major strength at Dovecote. The school has a number of opportunities for children to get involved with the running of their school (a student council, for example) and there are some compatible initiatives that all contribute to a supportive ethos. These practices are important because they communicate both care and an expectation of participation to the pupils.

Appointment of a co-ordinator

This role is essential to both the daily maintenance of a service and its long-term strategic development. Young mediators need regular support, a mechanism for identifying further training needs and opportunities to reflect on their practice with others. The co-ordinator needs to support the mediators, keep the service high profile and think a year or two in advance so that training cycles that guarantee the school retains a pool of trained mediators into the future are implemented.

Ensuring the service has a high profile

For peer mediation to be successful it has to be well used. For it to be well used it needs to be kept high profile. At Dovecote both the mediators and the service co-ordinator contribute to a number of activities (high visibility, assemblies, contributions to meetings) that do exactly this.

the stages of mediation accurately, the pupils are aware of the need to come down to the same level as the disputants, stay calm, make appropriate eye contact and speak confidently but softly.

The children trained as mediators feel the service has had a very positive impact on the school. They recognise that sometimes other pupils would rather talk to children of their own age about their problems, and that this saves teachers a lot of time.

> *You feel more comfortable with people of your own age. Teachers don't always go down to your level. Mediators give you more of a chance ... more of their time ...*
>
> *Year 5 pupil*

Mediators offer a patient approach that takes all children's problems very seriously. They also feel that the service intercepts problems at an early stage so they don't get any worse.

The success of peer mediation at Dovecote has not been without obstacles. Like a lot of services, they have struggled to recruit as many boys as girls. Unsurprisingly, the mediators recruited are not always perfectly behaved. Peer mediators are role models and it is key that this status is accompanied by generally good behaviour. However, Dovecote school has placed faith in one or two mediators who have themselves had difficulties. Tracey felt this was an important but delicate issue. She recognised that for the service to be respected by other pupils it needed to have a cross-section of the school community involved. This will include some pupils who are not perceived by others as the ones who always get things right. Tracey also recognised that mediators who encounter difficulties need support to apply the skills they've learned and employed with others to their own lives. This commitment has had a significant impact on one or two such individuals in particular.

Whereas the headteacher and link teacher have been fully committed from the onset, gaining other teachers' full understanding and support for the service wasn't easy at first. Tracey has adopted a patient and persistent approach which has been critical to success. She aims to keep the profile of the service continuously high. This is done by regular updates in staff meetings, frequent contributions to assemblies, a 'peer mediator of the week' award and a permanent display. Everybody is now fully aware of the service and teachers frequently refer pupils' conflicts to mediators.

The peer mediation service now manages itself to a large degree and is part of a network of wider support. The mediators have a weekly opportunity to meet socially for refreshments and to discuss specific issues, attend further training and manage the service. The school is also one of several schools in the area employing peer support. Links exist between these schools, and link teachers from each have the opportunity to meet, provide each other with support and share ideas.

The long-term future of the service is secured as a component of a broader school ethos. There are lots of school practices that complement peer mediation. These include a school council, a befriending scheme and opportunities for pupils to undertake jobs, including administrative tasks and gardening. There is a nurture group that addresses social and emotional aspects of learning for children in the early years and therapeutic support, including anger management training, is provided for individuals with additional needs. Children at Dovecote are thus seen holistically as members of a community with a valuable contribution to make to their school.

Sustaining peer mediation

Once a peer mediation scheme has been successfully introduced to a school, it is important to give a great deal of thought to how the service will be sustained into the future. With long-term planning a number of problems can be avoided. Steps such as developing a whole-school approach, gaining the support of staff, appointing a co-ordinator, maintaining the high profile of the service, monitoring and evaluating its impact, making links with other schools, allocating a budget and planning cycles of further training will all help sustain the service for years to come.

This chapter will start with a case study which describes how a peer mediation service has been sustained for several years at a primary school in Nottingham. In the following section key themes will be extracted to describe this good practice in more detail.

Case study – Dovecote Primary School

Dovecote is a large primary school in Nottingham with over 500 pupils. It has been running a successful peer mediation service for over three years – longer still considering that the school was formed by amalgamating three smaller schools, all of which had been running peer mediation services for approximately two years prior to the merger. Tracey Barton, a teacher at one of these schools, was eager to see the peer mediation services maintained, and volunteered to co-ordinate a service at the new school. Each of the former schools was consulted before amalgamation so the new service could draw upon the expertise already developed across the three sites. Peer mediation training was provided to the pupils by the local authority's Anti-Bullying Support (ABS) team. After the initial training, a relationship between the ABS team and a link teacher at the school was maintained. Tracey became the link teacher at Dovecote and now co-ordinates the service on a day-to-day basis. She keeps in regular contact with the ABS team, who sometimes provide further support and training when needed.

At Dovecote peer mediators are on duty at morning and afternoon playtimes, wearing bright yellow tops so they can be easily spotted. The mediators have identified certain 'hotspots' themselves and make sure they are close to these areas if needed. They offer a broad role; as well as providing mediation they look carefully for children who may be isolated and help them find friends to play with. The type of mediation they often provide is informal, on-the-spot help. The mediators are usually able to help other pupils progress through the stages of mediation: hearing each other's accounts of their dispute, hearing each other's feelings, generating alternative ideas to solve their problem and forming an agreement. More difficult conflicts are taken inside the school building, where a more formal process can be employed. The mediators are particularly well skilled in non-verbal communication as this formed part of their training. As well as being able to recall

Peer mediation log

Mediators	1	2
Disputants	1	2
Class		
Boy/girl		
Date		
Time		
Place		
What was the conflict about?		
Agreement		
Review date		

© *Mediation Matters LDA*

Summary

This chapter has discussed a number of important issues concerning the monitoring and evaluation of peer mediation in schools, such as carefully identifying the success criteria against which to assess the impact of the service realistically, and how to get mediators involved in the research process itself. In the next and final chapter I shall discuss what needs to be done to ensure the sustainability of a peer mediation service and use this as a means of summarising the whole book.

Approaches to evaluation

Evaluating the precise impact peer mediation has is not straightforward. Any peer mediator or teacher at a school where peer mediation has been successfully implemented will notice that things will feel very different, but they may not always be able to say exactly how or why. People researching peer mediation normally choose between positivistic approaches, which favour quantitative data-collection methods (e.g. collecting data on the number of conflicts referred to teachers for arbitration), or interpretivist approaches, which tend to favour qualitative data-collection methods (e.g. asking individuals to share their experiences). Both have their merits.

A positivistic approach will generate a breadth of information, usually statistical, but little depth. This approach assumes that the world consists of variables that can be measured and correlated to evaluate impact. Interventions and schools are complex systems and it is often not very easy to separate variables. The approach sometimes yields superficial data. It may tell us that peer mediation appears to be working, but not how and why. In contrast, an interpretivist approach will generate greater depth of information, which may be more informative but needs quite a lot of time to analyse. This approach places greater emphasis on people's experiences and their accounts. It is more subjective but tends to yield information that will be more useful to the ongoing monitoring, evaluation and further development of a peer mediation service. Given that peer mediation is underpinned by giving children a voice and a role, an interpretivist and qualitative approach is perhaps more consistent with its underlying philosophy.

A qualitative approach emphasises individuals' subjective experiences and allows them to share these experiences as part of the data-collection process. If you want to know how many people are using peer mediation, for what reasons, what agreements they establish and whether these are kept, then the easiest way to manage the data is for mediators to keep a detailed log.

The log provided (see p. 59) should be completed by mediators at the end of a session. It allows background information and details about the conflict to be recorded, and these can easily be reviewed for analysis of patterns at any time. At this stage simple recording of disputants' year groups, genders and other details may assist with the monitoring of equal opportunities. Whether the service is used more by girls than by boys, or younger rather than older pupils, can be assessed and, if deemed appropriate, steps can be identified to promote the service in different ways. The log also allows the agreement to be recorded. This has two benefits. Firstly, it facilitates the analysis of what kind of resolutions are being made and, if the service invites disputants back for a review, allows analysis of whether agreements are kept and for how long. Secondly, the agreement entry can be used to focus the disputants' attention on the agreement. They can even sign it as part of a promise to keep the agreement.

Another way of engaging participants in the process of monitoring and evaluation is to set up a research group. Many schools implementing peer mediation successfully and sustainably do this (see case study in Chapter 6). In such schools mediators meet weekly to debrief, share and discuss issues, suggest modifications and identify needs for further development, including their own training. This format is ideal for keeping informed in terms of what is and is not working well and responding promptly with appropriate developments. If these meetings are minuted, these records serve as evidence of ongoing review and development. As an example of best practice, the mediators could be charged with the responsibility of evaluating their own service. They could receive some further training in basic research methods to support this enhanced role. They could then design and implement their own data collection tools, such as questionnaires, and write an annual report for the school. Now, that's pupil empowerment!

It is also important to set realistic aims for a peer mediation service, and these should be proportionate to the investment of time and the resources allocated. Peer mediation is sometimes expected to have a dramatic impact on levels of aggression, violence and bullying within the school. Whereas this can certainly be achieved as part of a systematic whole-school approach that incorporates other elements (such as restorative approaches to behaviour management, challenging violence via the curriculum, opportunities for student voice and so on), it is too ambitious to expect this from a peer mediation service alone.

The table below summarises what it is reasonable to expect from a peer mediation service in terms of outcomes for mediators and schools. It also shows what can happen in supportive school environments and what should not be expected to happen.

Failure of the service to make an impact at any of these levels must be kept in perspective. If outcomes from tier 2 are not achieved, this raises issues about the school, its culture and the level of support for the service rather than about the peer mediation service itself. In this scenario, more will need to be done at a whole-school level to improve the impact the service has. If outcomes from tier 1 are not achieved, then the nature and quality of the training and service implementation need to be questioned, reviewed and ultimately improved.

Expectations of a peer mediation service

For peer mediators	For schools
Tier 1 – What should happen	
<ul><li>A greater understanding of conflict and its resolution</li><li>Enhanced verbal and non-verbal communication skills</li><li>Retention of the material covered in training</li><li>Increased confidence</li></ul>	<ul><li>Peer mediation is well used</li><li>Some conflicts will be prevented from escalating owing to early mediation</li><li>Reduced frequency of arbitration by teachers</li><li>Consideration of a greater range of problem-solving strategies</li><li>A high percentage of long-lasting agreements made</li></ul>
Tier 2 – What can happen in the right context	
<ul><li>Application of their communication and conflict resolution skills to their own lives and informal situations</li><li>Increased empathy for others</li></ul>	<ul><li>Calmer and more cohesive schools</li><li>More orderly starts to lessons</li><li>Teachers and other pupils using mediation skills</li><li>An increased awareness of what constitutes violent behaviour</li><li>Reductions in general aggression</li></ul>
Tier 3 – What should not be expected to happen	
<ul><li>Increased self-esteem</li><li>That peer mediators will not make mistakes in their own lives</li><li>That every mediation will result in an agreement</li></ul>	<ul><li>Dramatic reductions in general aggression, violence and exclusions from school</li><li>Direct improvements in attendance figures and test results</li><li>General improvements in personality traits such as self-esteem</li></ul>

5 Monitoring and evaluating peer mediation

School leaders, service co-ordinators and trainers will, quite rightly, want to monitor and evaluate their peer mediation service. It is important to know that considerable investments of time and resources are reaping dividends. It is perhaps even more important to learn along the way what is working well and what can be improved. In order to meet these aims it is essential that evaluation criteria, both summative and formative, are selected very carefully.

On what terms should peer mediation be evaluated?

The evaluations of many peer mediation services make the mistake of measuring outcomes that are not related to either the peer mediation training that has taken place or the aims of a peer mediation service. A common outcome measure used to examine the success of a peer mediation service is self-esteem. However, the nature of self-esteem and the purpose of measuring it are disputed. Firstly, the concept is somewhat problematic; some would argue that it is a rather fixed psychological category that is difficult to change. Others would argue that it is a value-free term. For example, it is possible to gain esteem from being a bully: 'I am the best bully in the school.' It cannot be assumed that high self-esteem equates with the confidence to apply peaceful conflict resolution or mediation skills. Other criteria not directly related to mediation such as exclusion rates, attendance figures and even test scores are sometimes erroneously used.

It is therefore helpful to reflect on what the core aspects of training to be a mediator and running a service are. The training involves developing teamwork, a greater understanding of conflict resolution strategies, and sophisticated communication skills that are used to help others. Therefore it is reasonable to expect that peer mediators retain their knowledge about conflict, are able to identify many different ways to resolve conflict, can demonstrate active listening skills, and can make disputants feel comfortable and guide them towards achieving an agreement. It may also be reasonable to expect them to gain some confidence with these communication skills and apply them to their own lives with practice and support.

More generally, the aims of a peer mediation service include providing peer support and guidance to those who have already experienced a problem, with the aim of helping them reach a mutually satisfying agreement before the situation escalates. Hence it is reasonable to expect a peer mediation service to be well used by other pupils and for the process to be successful. This success should have a positive impact on the number of problems referred to teachers and the number of arguments that escalate. As part of a whole-school approach, it is reasonable to expect a calmer and more cohesive school. It is upon these criteria that peer mediation should be evaluated.

- When disputants can't think of ideas for an agreement. Mediators can consider offering disputants a break and returning later. Alternatively, they can invite the disputants to list all their ideas. Mediators may make an initial suggestion as this may help disputants think of others, which may be particularly helpful for younger children.
- When they don't think an agreement will be kept. Mediators can invite them back for a review after a short period of time.

Peer mediators should be reminded that most of the scenarios they mediate will be quite straightforward. However, it is good to be prepared. 'What ifs' and ways to respond should be discussed during additional training and as necessary when mediators meet. It is a good idea to start an advice booklet for mediators in which strategies that have been successful are recorded. This could be added to any other resources available for mediators.

Summary

Part II has provided a detailed account of the peer mediation training process. This chapter has shared an overview of the further training mediators require in order to perform this role for their school. The chapter has also reviewed a number of issues to consider during both mediator training and the early stages of implementing a service. In Part III our attention turns to how to monitor, evaluate and sustain a peer mediation service.

Occasions when a mediator should ask another mediator to mediate on their behalf:

- When a mediator is a good friend of either of the disputants.
- When a mediator was involved in the incident.
- When a mediator witnessed the incident and this might influence their guidance.
- If a disputant asks for a change of mediator for an appropriate reason.

Occasions when mediators will need to remind disputants of the ground rules:

- When stories contradict and this is preventing progress. The mediators should remind the disputants that they must both want to solve the problem and invite them to elaborate on their accounts. Disputants could be seen individually if this continues to be an obstacle; this may help them speak more easily.
- When disputants interrupt each other, do not use each other's names, blame each other or do not follow the ground rules. The mediators should remind disputants about the rules and ask them if they still accept these and wish to continue.

Occasions when mediation should be stopped:

- When one or both parties fail to keep the ground rules despite several reminders. They should be thanked for coming, told the reason that mediation has been stopped and invited back another day.
- When a disputant is in distress. This may be because they are still upset, they are there against their will or they are intimidated by the other disputant. There are three options: mediators can stop mediation, offer individual mediation, or invite them back at a later date.
- When a disputant is still very angry. Mediators can invite them back when they feel ready or offer them a short break.
- When the dispute concerns a very serious matter or a serious disclosure is made (such as a child protection issue, criminal behaviour, drug-taking, a serious assault or persistent bullying). The mediators will need to stop the mediation, explain why and refer to a teacher. The possibility of this happening should be explained in advance.
- When one party doesn't want to mediate or solve the problem. They should be told why mediation has been stopped and invited to come back if they change their mind.
- When agreement can't be reached, which will happen on occasion. In this case they should be invited to return in a few days after a break, or if they have new ideas for an agreement.

Occasions when mediators may need to think creatively:

- When a disputant changes their story or two versions of a story are very different. Mediators will need to consider whether this is a change or a development. If it is definitely a change, they should state this and ask for clarification. Also, mediators should remind the disputants of the need to stay focused on a solution.
- When other people become implicated in the problem. If there is an issue that can be resolved there and then, mediation should proceed. If this is not possible, mediators should ask disputants what they want to do. If possible they can come back with the others and continue. If not, mediators should evaluate whether any issues can be resolved between those who have volunteered.
- When lots of issues are raised. Mediators should consider writing them down. Disputants should agree on a focus, and not bring anything else up until these issues are resolved. Mediators can also consider meeting more than once, perhaps with different focuses.

Training for other key people

Tyrrell (2002) argues that it is essential that adult members of staff, including lunchtime supervisors, receive training in both how to support the peer mediation service and how to use non-confrontational behaviour management techniques. At an early stage peer mediators should be given an opportunity to demonstrate their new skills to teachers, support staff and other pupils. This simultaneously advertises the service and increases understanding about how mediation works and how it should be used. Although peer mediators take a large degree of responsibility for running their own service, teachers and lunchtime supervisors often act as gatekeepers and are needed on board to ensure that the service runs smoothly, and that appropriate conflicts are referred to mediation. As discussed previously, there needs to be some consistency between the communication practices of staff members and those underpinning mediation.

Managing the early stages

Once the training is completed, most peer mediation takes place at lunch and playtimes, usually in a quiet room or in designated areas outside (Cremin 2001). Tyrrell (2002) describes how rotas can be drawn up by or for pupils to schedule mediation duties. A peer mediation log (see p. 59) can also be made during peer mediation and kept for future reference. Mediation is a voluntary process for all (Isenhart and Spangle 2000); therefore services have a greater chance of being well used if they are very high profile. Strategies to raise the profile of peer mediation services include advertising the service widely, periodic class and school assemblies and mediators wearing baseball caps or something similar to make themselves visible (Sellman 2002).

The smooth running of a peer mediation service will benefit from the following first steps:

- appointing a teacher to help co-ordinate the service;
- arranging regular meetings for the mediators to review the service and receive top-up training if necessary;
- dedicating a quiet and private space for mediation to take place;
- drawing up a rota of peer mediators (ideally there should be at least one pair of peer mediators inside to help pupils and another pair on each playground to escort pupils wanting mediation inside);
- making mediators easily identifiable by wearing caps or something similar;
- formalising a protocol for mediators to get help from adults if needed;
- establishing a peer mediation log so that agreements are recorded;
- giving the service a high profile;
- supporting the service with staff training.

What ifs

The focus of peer mediation training is about practice and achieving confidence. Part of this process needs to include what to do in problematic situations. Most matters brought to mediation should be straightforward to resolve as most pupils want to reach an agreement and restore their friendships. However, mediators need to be prepared to deal with the occasional difficulty, such as when a dispute is inappropriate for mediation or disputants don't follow the ground rules. Peer mediators will need to know what to do in these situations and how to stop mediation if necessary.

Mediators will benefit from further support and training in this regard during the first few months of the service. Lampen and Lampen (1997) have produced a booklet on this topic which contains many suggestions from mediators themselves. This guidance underpins the four sets of occasions that follow.

Problem scenarios for peer mediation

Disputant – keep changing your story

Mediator – take sides with one of the disputants

Disputant – keep interrupting the other disputant

Mediator – start telling one of the disputants what to do

Disputant – make personal remarks about the other disputant

Disputant – start arguing with the other disputant

Disputants – you haven't really got a dispute and you're just here to waste the mediators' time

Mediator – pretend you have seen the dispute and start telling them what you saw

Disputant – mention something that is too serious for mediation

Disputants – neither of you can think of any ideas for an agreement

Stages of peer mediation

Cut up the cards and shuffle them. Pupils work together to sort them into the correct order.

Introduce themselves

Agree to the ground rules

Define the problem in turns and in their own words

Explore each other's wants, needs and feelings

Generate potential solutions

Agree a solution

Session 5

1 Opening game

Play Fruit Salad (see p. 32) or a game of your choice.

2 Activity

Divide the pupils into random pairs, then 4s. Mediators refamiliarise themselves with scripts and disputants decide upon a conflict. After one basic practice, give one person in each group a piece of paper outlining a problem (see p. 51). Watch problem peer mediations and see if the circle can identify the problem and suggest coping strategies. Discuss good practice.

3 Closing game

Play Bounce and Catch (see p. 36) or a game of your choice.

Session 6

1 Opening game

Vote for and play the group's favourite game.

2 Activity

Continue to practise problem mediations from the previous session.

3 Discussion

Discuss what went well and what could be improved.

4 Question and answer session

This is an opportunity for pupils to ask questions about how the service will be run. It should be attended by the service co-ordinator if they are not already present. This part of the session can also be used to plan how the service will operate.

5 Round

Each group member introduces the person on their left: 'This is … and they will make a good peer mediator because …'

6 Final activity

Present certificates. It is important to close the training and celebrate success.

Session 4

1 Opening game

Play Back-to-Back Drawings. Pupils sit in pairs with their backs to each other. Each has a pencil and paper. One pupil draws a simple line drawing. They then describe it in as much detail as they can for their partner to draw. They then swap roles.

2 Round

'Something I did well last time was …'

3 Activity

Share with a partner extensions to the following statements: 'A time when I felt angry was …', 'A time when I felt anxious was …', 'A time when I felt happy was …'. The partner is to repeat back as accurately as they can. They then swap roles.

4 Discussion

How did it feel to share feelings? Why is confidentiality important? Why is it important to share feelings? What is the purpose of sharing feelings during peer mediation?

Note: Peer mediators need reminding that they are offering a confidential service, and they should be clear about both what this means and exceptions when confidentiality can't be kept (e.g. if a child protection issue, criminality or other very serious behaviour is disclosed). They will need to remind disputants about confidentiality during the introduction to mediation, when the rules are agreed. Mediators should also be trained to halt the process if a disclosure occurs and advise disputants about what will happen next.

Mediators

Disputants

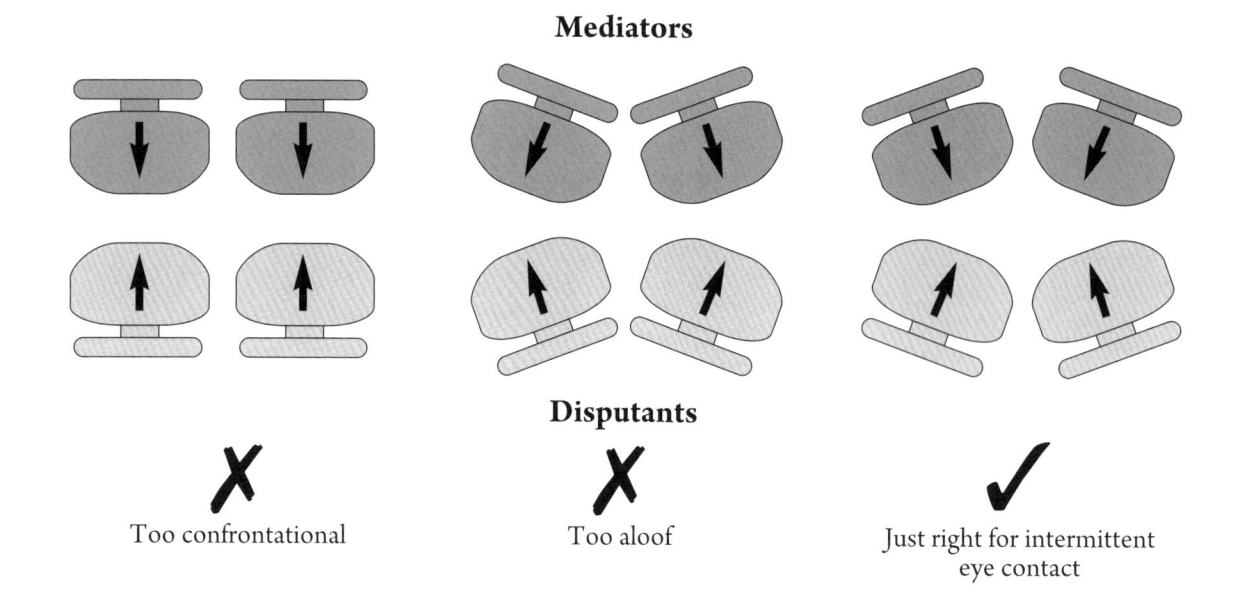

✗ Too confrontational   ✗ Too aloof   ✓ Just right for intermittent eye contact

Session 3

1 Opening game
Play Guess the Leader (see p. 31) or a game of your choice.

2 Activity
Get into pairs of mediators and disputants. Mediators read through scripts (see pp. 43–44), and disputants devise a conflict scenario typical for pupils at the school. Check understanding of scripts and appropriateness of disputes. Put pairs into 4s, then practise and demonstrate to the rest of the group. Repeat the process with roles swapped over. Practise again and demonstrate to the rest of group.

3 Discussion
Discuss each demonstration. Invite pupils to identify three positive features and one suggestion for improvement.

4 Round
'Something I've enjoyed today is …'

5 Closing game
Vote for and play the group's favourite game.

> Note: At this stage the conflict scenarios selected need to be both sensible and straightforward to resolve. There must also be consistency between disputants. Those adopting the role of disputant often try and make it too realistic, and hence too difficult, for mediators to practise. Remind the pupils of the need to keep it simple so that basic mediation can be practised first.

PART II: IMPLEMENTING PEER MEDIATION

Session 1

Opening game
Play Waves (see p. 35) or a game of your choice.

Round
'I'm … and I'm pleased to be here because …'

Ground rules
Recap the group contract written during Session 2 of initial training (p. 31).

Activity
Get into groups using jigsaws or coloured dots. Choose one of the conflict cartoons (p. 40) and answer the following questions: What happened before? What does each party want/feel? What choices will make the situation worse? What choices will make the situation better? Report back to the whole group and scribe lists of things that escalate and de-escalate conflict.

Closing game
Play Keeper of the Keys (see p. 33) or a game of your choice.

Session 2

Opening game
Play Spin the Frisbee (see p. 30) or a game of your choice.

Activity
Observe a demonstration of peer mediation. As in initial training, it is preferable to watch experienced mediators if this is possible. Discuss what children notice about the process. Discuss seating arrangements and body language. Get into groups and resequence the stages of mediation (see p. 50).

Closing game
Play Affirmation Detective (see p. 34) or a game of your choice.

Note: It's important to go over how to set out the chairs (see p. 47). This should allow both mediators and disputants to maintain eye contact with each other without being intimidated, so a diagonal formation is best. This is an ideal opportunity to recap listening skills and non-verbal communication.

Example of a training programme

There now follows an example of a training programme in mediation skills. There are six sessions, each lasting between one and two hours, which should ideally be delivered intensively over two whole days. Like the initial training programme in the previous chapter, this is a guide that should be adapted for the needs of the group to be trained. There is a lot of material to cover in the allocated time as the pupils need to be ready to mediate others by the end of the programme. Hence communication skills and opportunities for practice form a considerable part of the training.

The central skill peer mediators use is active listening. This process involves listening to information with care and a great deal of concentration. This information is then repeated back to the speaker as accurately as possible, sometimes in a more concise manner. The listener should also check they have understood. For example:

Disputant   Well I was sitting next to A and I turned around to talk to B, then I turned back and my pencil had gone missing and I looked across the classroom and I saw C with the same pencil and I went up to him and asked him for my pencil back but he said it was his.

Mediator   **So, you were talking to B and when you turned round your pencil wasn't there. You saw C with the same pencil and asked him for it back but he said it was his. Is that correct? Have I understood?**

Peer mediators should be very careful not to change the words or meaning when they repeat back. Experienced mediators may be able to ask for clarification or more information should they feel it appropriate, but they should not put words in the disputants' mouths. The process works because disputants have the opportunity to hear each other's accounts, feelings and suggested solutions. The emphasis is on the disputants identifying these solutions themselves and the role of the mediator is to facilitate rather than direct this process.

The aims of all sessions are:
- to develop understanding of the nature of conflict and its resolution;
- to practise peer mediation;
- to develop a range of strategies to cope with difficult mediations.

▶▶▶ **Peer mediator 2** [B's name], how did you feel at the time and how do you feel now?

So you felt ...

Peer mediator 1 It is important to acknowledge how the other person is feeling.

[A's name], how is [B's name] feeling?

So [B's name] feels ...

Peer mediator 2 [B's name], how is [A's name] feeling?

So [A's name] feels ...

Peer mediator 1 Here's a reminder. We would really like you to think of some ideas for yourself and agree a solution between yourselves. Please ask for ideas if you can't think of any.

[A's name], what would you like to happen to sort this problem out?

So you would like ...

Peer mediator 2 [B's name], what would you like to happen to sort this problem out?

So you would like ...

Peer mediator 1 [A's name], is this idea acceptable to you?

(If not: What changes would you like to make? ... and repeat question)

Peer mediator 2 [B's name], is this idea acceptable to you?

(If not: What changes would you like to make? ... and repeat question)

Peer mediator 1 Thank you for working together to solve this problem successfully.

Peer mediator 2 Please come back to peer mediation next time you have a problem.

Peer mediation script

Peer mediator 1   Hello. Are you both ready to begin mediation?

Peer mediator 2   Please tell us your names.
My name is ... and this is ...

Peer mediator 1   Thank you for both coming to peer mediation. We are here to help you think of a solution to your problem. We stay impartial (meaning we do not take sides) and unless you say something very serious, we will keep your confidence (meaning we won't tell other pupils your secrets).

Peer mediator 2   Please use these guidelines: use each other's name, avoid saying anything that may upset or blame the other person and listen to each other in turn. You both must want to solve the problem.

Do you both agree to follow these guidelines?

Peer mediator 1   [A's name], please tell us in your own words what happened.

So this is what happened ...

Have I understood?

Peer mediator 2   [B's name], please tell us in your own words what happened.

So this is what happened ...

Have I understood?

Peer mediator 1   [A's name], how did you feel at the time and how do you feel now?

So you felt ...

▶▶▶

PART II: IMPLEMENTING PEER MEDIATION

These are set out in a script used by pairs of peer mediators (see pp. 43–44).

Peer mediation scripts play an important role in a successful service. They are extremely useful in training, helping pupils to remember the stages of mediation and prompting them to ask the right questions at the right time. Most pupils will also want to use the scripts for the first few weeks of their duty, and this is encouraged. Mediators shouldn't become too dependent on scripts, though. They need to internalise the stages of mediation and the types of questions to ask as well as knowing how to respond to the unexpected. As mediators gain experience and grow in confidence, this transference should happen quite naturally.

As an illustration, the following sequence is an extract from an interview with a 10-year-old mediator who had been trained seven weeks earlier. She recounts how she has appropriated the language of the script into her everyday language, which she sometimes uses in other difficult situations.

Researcher **What kinds of conflict did you experience before being trained as a peer mediator?**

Pupil Usually a lot of people arguing and shouting at each other and nobody knowing what to do with everybody standing in the background unsure of what to do, so the fight would go on and get worse.

Researcher **Would you have been one of those standing in the background?**

Pupil Yes, because I wouldn't know what to do.

Researcher **And has that changed at all?**

Pupil I'm now trying to sort out problems before they get too violent.

Researcher **How do you do that?**

Pupil Well, I ask them to calm down and ask them the different questions and try to make them see that it's not what they think it is and that it's different and then they should see that it's not a fighting matter and should make friends.

Researcher **And what questions do you use?**

Pupil I ask them what's happened ... and then I ask them to explain what's happened, the other person explains what's happened and then think about the two things that they've said and then give them a few ideas and think about what to do next.

Researcher **Where do those questions come from?**

Pupil The scripts, I use some of the words that are on the script.

Researcher **When do you use those scripts?**

Pupil When we're peer mediating at the moment, but we usually remember them and we use them outside as well.

Although a script is provided, there is no reason why mediators can't write their own. In fact, this is a very good idea as it reinforces the stages of mediation and frames the questions in language that other pupils will easily understand. Some support should be given during the writing process to ensure all the stages are included and the questions are framed using positive language.

4 Implementing a peer mediation service

Pupils who are to become peer mediators will require additional training in communication skills, establishing and maintaining ground rules, guiding the process and dealing with 'problem' mediations. All of these aspects are discussed in detail in this chapter, which also includes an example of a further training programme. Particular attention is paid to the skill of active listening, and a mediation script is provided which can be used by mediators as a guide during training and the early days of the service. Advice about how to manage the early stages of a mediation service is also included.

Further training

After the satisfactory completion of preliminary training, pupils should be invited to participate in a minimum of six additional training sessions in mediation skills. As peer mediation services usually involve the commitment of spare time (break and lunchtimes), pupils should be asked to volunteer. Schools may want to consider how they will recruit and select a cohort of pupils from those who have been trained so far. Some schools invite pupils to write letters of application outlining what they have learned and what they may contribute to the service. Another idea is to ask pupils to nominate whom they think will make good candidates as peer mediators should be good role models. The case study in Chapter 6 has more information about how to select peer mediators.

Research by Tyrrell (2002) has identified that mediation for children is not the same as for adults. Children need additional training in such sophisticated skills as staying neutral in disputes and repeating back rather than reframing what has been heard, and in the importance of ensuring confidentiality. Although teachers are often amazed by the skills trained mediators demonstrate, pupils find the support of a script very helpful, at least during the early stages of running the service.

Peer mediation scripts

The bulk of further training in peer mediation should be dedicated to practising peer mediation in a range of situations with the aid of a script.

The process of peer mediation has four distinct stages. These are:
- setting the scene, explaining the process and agreeing to the ground rules;
- hearing both sides of the story, with an emphasis on how each person is feeling;
- generating possible solutions to the dispute;
- an agreement.

Conflict cartoons

The fable of the two mules

© The Religious Society of Friends in Britain

© Mediation Matters LDA

When you … I feel …

When you		I feel	
	tell lies about me		
	include me in a game		
	make a joke about me		
	offer to help me		
	put me down		
	share something with me		
	threaten to hurt me		
	whisper in front of me		
	say nice things about me		

Session 9

Aim

- To review learning from previous sessions and affirm each other.

Programme

1 Welcome

Introduce aims and agenda.

2 Opening game

Vote for and play the group's favourite game.

3 Round

'Something that I've learned during training is …'

4 Activity

In groups compile a list of ways of ending a conflict without hurting others, recalling discussions from previous sessions. Share them together and give out a prize if a group thinks of more than twenty.

5 Discussion

Provide an overview of the process for volunteering for and taking part in further training (to be a peer mediator), then provide an opportunity for questions and answers.

6 Affirmation activity

Ask everyone to write their name on a sheet of paper, then walk around the classroom and write anonymous affirmations on each other's sheets.

7 Round

Pupils should share something from their sheet with the rest of the circle.

8 Closing game

Play Keeper of the Keys (see p. 33).

Note: Additional sessions can be added to extend or revisit any of the core activities.

PART II: IMPLEMENTING PEER MEDIATION

4 Activity

Set up a tableau. Choose one of the conflict scenarios discussed and ask two or three volunteers to stand in the positions shown on the picture, as statues. Share ideas about ways of ending conflict without anyone being hurt by moving the figures in the tableau to new positions. This is an ideal opportunity to explore personal space, aggressive and passive stances, gestures and eye contact.

5 Closing game

Pass two tambourines around the circle in opposite directions, making as little noise as possible. Discuss whether the group has improved since Session 2.

Session 8

Aim

- To explore ways of ending conflicts without anyone getting hurt.

Programme

1 Welcome

Introduce aims and agenda.

2 Opening game

Using feet only, pass two balloons or large cans around the circle in opposite directions without touching the floor.

3 Discussion

Read out the list from Session 7 of different ways of ending a conflict without hurting others. Can anyone think of any more?

4 Activity

In groups ask the pupils to choose one of the conflict scenarios from Session 7 for a role-play, then agree on characters, history and a trigger to the conflict. They should devise a way of finishing the conflict without anyone getting hurt (use the list from session 7 if necessary) and present to the rest of the group.

5 Closing game

Play Bounce and Catch. Bounce a ball to someone in the circle. When they catch it they must say something positive about themselves, such as something they are good at. Continue until everyone has had a turn. A variation would be for the person bouncing the ball to say something affirming about the person they are bouncing it to.

2 Opening game

Play Waves. Put three empty chairs at different places in the circle and give the instruction that when there is a spare place on your left you have to move into it – this creates a wave pattern. Somebody then stands in the middle and has to find a seat while the rest of the class are moving round. When this is done successfully, choose someone else to stand in the middle for a turn.

3 Activity

Ask groups to look at a selection of pictures showing a range of scenarios involving people in conflict or co-operation. You could use newspaper or magazine cuttings, or SEAL resources (DfES 2005). Ask groups to sort them into two sets (conflict and co-operation), then look at those images that depict conflict. Ask groups to discuss and record: 'How is each person feeling?', 'What do they want to happen?' Groups should feed back to the whole group and discuss how this relates to peer mediation. Begin to discuss the choices each person has.

4 Closing game

Play Emotions. A volunteer makes their face and body show a chosen emotion. The group tries to guess the emotion. If anyone guesses correctly, they can have a turn. To extend the activity, the guesser could suggest a situation that could make them feel that emotion.

Session 7

Aim

- To continue to explore feelings associated with conflicts.
- To explore choices available in a conflict situation.

Programme

1 Welcome

Introduce aims and agenda.

2 Opening game

Play Fruit Salad (see p. 32).

3 Discussion

Put children into groups of 4 or 5. Give each group an image depicting at least one pupil in conflict (p. 40). Discuss and record:
- What might have happened before?
- What choices does each person in the picture have?
- Which choices will result in a constructive or a destructive ending?

Each group is to feed back and make a list together of the constructive ways to end conflict.

PART II: IMPLEMENTING PEER MEDIATION

Session 5

Aim

- To continue to develop understanding of working co-operatively.
- To explore contexts associated with feelings.

Programme

Welcome
Introduce aims and agenda.

Opening game
Play Guess the Leader (see p. 31).

Activity
In advance photocopy 'The fable of the two mules' (p. 39) onto an assortment of different coloured card. Cut each card into horizontal strips so the story can be jumbled up and resequenced. Ask groups to order the pictures from the story. Share the story with the whole group, discuss its meaning and evaluate how the task was completed.

Discussion
Ask groups to discuss the question 'What things, people and situations make me feel angry/happy/sad/frightened?' Report back and discuss the things people do to manage their feelings.

Closing game
Play Affirmation Detective. A pupil is blindfolded and has to guess whom the group is talking about when they share positive comments.

Session 6

Aim

- To explore feelings associated with conflicts.

Programme

Welcome
Introduce aims and agenda.

Session 4

Aims

- To develop an understanding of how feelings are linked to contexts/actions.
- To understand the skills involved in active listening.

Programme

1 Welcome

Introduce aims and agenda. Discuss group contract and display.

2 Communication activity

The class forms two concentric circles, each person facing a partner, which rotate between each exchange. Each pair of pupils shares an account of a time when each felt happy, then a time when each felt frightened, then a time when each felt proud. Feed back about feelings and contexts, then discuss 'What makes listening easier?'

3 Activity

Type a list of pairs (e.g. salt and pepper, table and chair) onto individual cards. Pupils use these to find a partner. Ask pairs to complete the 'When you … I feel …' worksheet (p. 38). Use the emotional vocabulary word bank from Session 3 for ideas if necessary. Feed back and discuss the range of feelings associated with each action.

4 Round

'Something that makes me happy is …'

5 Closing game

Play Keeper of the Keys. A volunteer is blindfolded and sits in the middle of the circle with a bunch of keys underneath their chair. A child is chosen to try to take the keys as quietly as possible. If the child on the chair hears them and points to them, they go back to their place and someone else has a turn. If they successfully take the keys, they have the next turn on the chair.

Session 3

Aims

- To continue to develop teamwork within the group and to identify those choices that will help our group work well together.
- To develop an emotional vocabulary.

Programme

1 Welcome

Introduce aims and agenda. Review draft group contract.

2 Opening game

Play Fruit Salad. Give everyone in the circle the name of one of four different fruits. One person stands in the middle and calls out one of the fruits. Everyone who is that fruit swaps places and the person in the middle tries to sit down, leaving somebody new in the middle. If the person says 'Fruit salad', everybody swaps places.

3 Activity

Put children into groups using jigsaws (cut picture postcards into several pieces, give these out randomly and pupils use the pieces to get into groups and complete the jigsaws). Give each group a set of images of children displaying a range of emotions. These could be from SEAL resources (DfES 2005) or magazine cuttings. Ask the children to put them into a feelings line – for example, anger or sadness to anxiety to happiness – then choose a photo from the beginning, middle and end and make lists of as many words as possible that describe those feelings. Groups then report back. Keep the words as a word bank for the next session.

4 Round

'Something I've seen [name] do well is …'

5 Closing game

Play Pass the Emotion. A child makes a face to show an emotion at a child sitting next to them. They pass the emotion round the circle.

Session 2

Aims

- To continue to develop teamwork within the group.
- To identify those choices that will help our group work together well.

Programme

1 Welcome

Introduce aims and agenda.

2 Opening game

Play Guess the Leader. One child (the guesser) closes their eyes while a leader is chosen. The leader starts an action such as clapping which the other children copy. The leader can change the action whenever they like: e.g. tapping knees, clicking fingers. The guesser has three guesses to identify the leader.

3 Activity

Use playing cards to get the pupils into random groups (pupils have to get into groups with others of the same number or same suit). Ask each group to identify five characteristics of a group that works well together, then feed back to the whole group, sharing the ideas and agreeing on them to establish a draft group contract.

4 Round

Pupils set themselves individual targets from the group contract and share in a round.

5 Closing game

Pass two tambourines around the circle in opposite directions, making as little noise as possible.

Note: Establishing a group contract may take some time, but is an essential first step. Pupils are likely to suggest rules themselves similar to those of mediation, and may refer to areas such as listening, body language, respect and feelings. It is important to do this near the beginning of the training because it gives the group an opportunity to define the criteria via which the group will manage itself.

PART II: IMPLEMENTING PEER MEDIATION

Session 1

Aims

- To develop teamwork within the group.
- To introduce the aims of the training programme.

Programme

1 Welcome

Ask the group to sit in a circle. Everyone shares their name and a fact about themselves.

2 Opening game

Play Spin the Frisbee. One person goes to the middle of the circle and spins a frisbee or plastic plate on its edge while calling out the name of a classmate, who must pick up the frisbee before it stops spinning. See how many children can have a turn before someone lets it fall.

3 Discussion

What can we do to make games and activities work well? Introduce a stop/quiet signal (e.g. raised hand) to gain attention.

4 Activity

Introduce the main aims of the project: to develop conflict resolution skills and set up a peer mediation service. Observe a peer mediation demonstration (this could be done by mediators from another year group or school, or showing a video). In groups list the skills observed and then share them with the whole group. List these under the headings of **co-operation**, **communication** and **affirmation** skills, explaining the meaning of each. When discussing communication skills, make sure non-verbal skills are discussed, such as refined but relaxed body posture, eye contact, mirroring body positions and displaying visual cues that reassure others that they are being listened to.

5 Co-operative activity

Print the key words (**co-operation**, **communication** and **affirmation**) onto coloured card in a large font size and cut out the individual letters (one letter per piece of card, one colour per word). Give these out and ask the group to work together to make the words.

6 Closing round

'Something I've enjoyed today is …'

Note: It is important to observe peer mediation at the beginning of the training programme. It shows that children can mediate between others, it stimulates motivation, and it identifies an outcome to work towards and a clear context for the practice of key skills.

Communication

Pupils can practise a range of talking and listening exercises during circle time. Rounds provide opportunities for them to introduce themselves and their favourite things (such as colour, food or role models) or respond to different scenarios (such as 'when … I feel …'). Quizzes after rounds encourage good listening. It is very important that pupils have plenty of opportunities to listen and repeat back accurately because as peer mediators they will need these skills perhaps more than any others. Such activities benefit from reflection afterwards. For example, the group should be able to identify a collective list of the qualities of good talking and listening, which can be kept and used for future reference.

Co-operation

There are numerous games to play during circle time to develop co-operation skills. These include passing objects (e.g. passing a noisy object quietly or a difficult object such as a large tin can with your feet) or solving puzzles in small teams (e.g. jigsaws made out of postcards).

Co-operative skills can be focused by controlling the elements of each activity. For example, groups solving puzzles without talking concentrates their attention on communicating in different ways as a group. Whenever pupils get into groups there is an opportunity for a co-operation exercise. Pupils can be given something such as a playing card, jigsaw piece or coloured dot, and then form a group by finding children with items that match their own.

Sample scheme of work

The initial training can be delivered over nine sessions. The sessions could take place in PSHE or citizenship curriculum time, or another suitable timetable slot. Each session lasts one to two hours and contains a range of games and activities to develop the skills of affirmation, communication and co-operation, plus a core activity designed to increase knowledge and understanding of conflict and mediation. The programme is provided as a guide only and should be adapted to the needs of the group being trained.

Key skills

It is helpful to think of introductory (whole-class) peer mediation training as an iceberg (see below). Using a problem-solving approach to resolve conflict successfully is just the tip of the iceberg. Such an approach is underpinned by a number of key attributes and skills hidden beneath the surface: knowledge and understanding of conflict, a commitment to non-violence and the skills of affirmation, communication and co-operation.

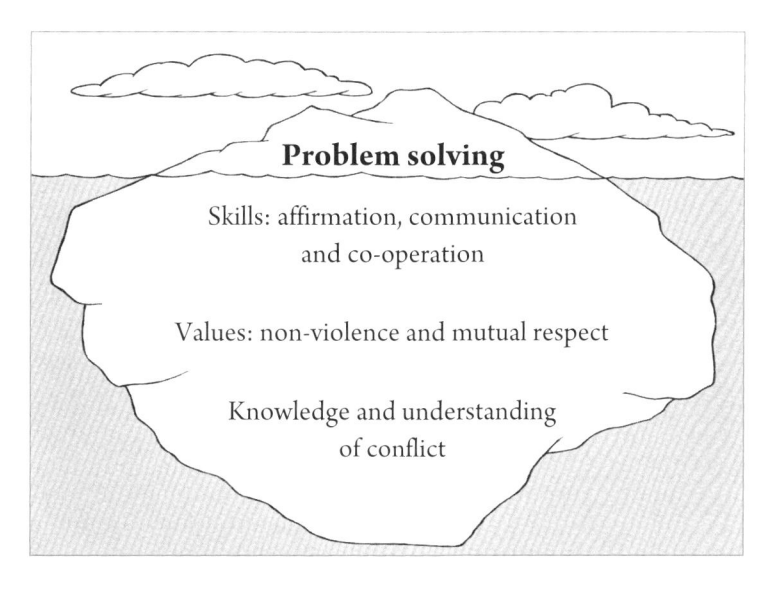

Problem solving

Skills: affirmation, communication and co-operation

Values: non-violence and mutual respect

Knowledge and understanding of conflict

Introductory training activities in conflict resolution skills and peer mediation, delivered via circle time, emphasise one or more of these elements.

Knowledge and understanding of conflict

If pupils are to help others to solve their problems they will need to possess a basic understanding of conflict, how it is informed by the past and people's different feelings, what options are available to disputants, and how to help effectively. Time should be allocated within initial training to teach this. Mediators will also need a sound emotional vocabulary as well as an understanding of how conflict can be escalated/de-escalated and how certain courses of action are more likely to result in win–win outcomes.

Values: non-violence and mutual respect (affirmation)

For peer mediation to be successful, it is essential that both mediators and their clients accept and agree to abide by a number of ground rules. These normally include showing each other respect and genuinely wanting to solve the problem. Pupils need to understand that they have various options available to them and that they should seek those that are going to be acceptable to both sides. Violence is therefore not an option. Activities designed to develop the skill of affirmation are an important means of facilitating respect for self and others.

Affirmation is the ability to recognise the positive qualities about yourself and others. The first step in developing affirmation is to build up a sense of personal identity that is both positive and accurate. The second step for many schoolchildren is overcoming the embarrassment of saying and recognising positive things about themselves and each other. Many children who have experienced little praise and warmth can find this difficult; thus the affirmation needs to be given and taken genuinely.

if a service has already been introduced. Providing training at this age allows pupils plenty of time to undertake their role for the school before they leave for secondary school at the age of 11. They can also assist with subsequent cycles of training by providing demonstrations and support to future trainees. At secondary school children from any year group can be trained to mediate. However, it may make sense to identify at least two pools of trainees to mediate younger and older pupils. Secondary schools frequently inherit pupils from their feeder schools who are already trained mediators and they should provide an opportunity for them to continue to use their skills if they so wish. There is more information about choosing who is to carry out peer mediator training on page 41 and in the case study on page 60.

The school will also need to make the important decision concerning whether to train mediators themselves or with the support and expertise of external training, provided by either the local authority or one of many independent specialist training providers throughout the country. There are a number of significant advantages in commissioning an external training provider. Although this may be expensive, their expertise is invaluable as peer mediation involves an array of subtle yet sophisticated skills. External training also brings status to the training and the eventual service. The aim of any relationship with a training provider should be to transfer expertise to the school so it can become self-sufficient. Many training organisations plan for such transference by providing training for specialist teachers and also offer ongoing support.

Training as a process

To establish a peer mediation service pupils need training in foundational conflict resolution skills, then mediation. This is often delivered in two distinct stages. In Stage 1 (this chapter) pupils receive introductory training in conflict resolution skills and are shown the mediation process. This should ideally be delivered to whole classes. Following Stage 1 training pupils can nominate themselves or others for further training. In Stage 2 (Chapter 4) formal peer mediation training takes place. It is important that pupils are given enough time to complete their Stage 2 training (ten hours' minimum), to perform the role of peer mediator (for, ideally, at least one academic year) and perhaps assist in training others.

Peer mediation training is often delivered via circle time which involves the whole class or a group sitting in a circle. At any time everybody can see each other in the circle. This creates an environment suitable for a number of co-operative activities and group discussion. Morris (1999) argues that circle time is an ideal format for managing the social dynamics of a classroom and developing a co-operative group. One of the strengths of circle time is that it develops a group's ability to reflect on the success of activities and the well-being of their peers. It does this by making the group equally responsible for their own cohesion and achievement. Critiques of circle time (e.g. Lang 1998) have highlighted the fact that activities have to be very well planned in order to achieve intended learning objectives. However, the role of the teacher is that of a facilitator and they should not completely dominate the agenda. Through careful questioning, pupils can be encouraged to identify the skills being practised and the social learning taking place. Useful reflective questions to ask during circle-time sessions include these:

- What happened during that activity?
- What did you see others doing well?
- What needs to happen for this to work better next time?
- Why was it important to …?
- In what ways could this be important for a peer mediator?

PART II: IMPLEMENTING PEER MEDIATION

Peer mediation training

All peer mediators need to develop a range of skills, which usually requires specialist training. A problem-solving approach to conflict resolution is underpinned by knowledge and understanding of conflict as well as skills in affirmation, communication and co-operation. Each of these key skills will be discussed in this chapter and an example of a training programme will be shared. Before training can commence a school will need to decide how best to start, which is where this chapter also begins.

Starting points

To get to the point where a peer mediation service is up and running, a school must make a number of practical decisions, such as these:

- Who will be selected for training?
- How will they be selected?
- When will the training begin?
- Does the school have sufficient expertise to train pupils themselves or does it need to employ an external agency?
- How and when will the service operate?

Pupils are normally selected for peer mediation training during the later years of their primary education or at any time during their secondary education. They usually mediate children of the same age or younger and work in pairs or small teams. Stacey et al. (1997) give one example of children as young as 6 being trained as peer mediators. However, the type of mediation provided is limited to listening to each other's feelings and agreeing on simple solutions. Older children are more able to provide a neutral and non-judgemental service. Most pupils aged 10 and above can easily help other children understand the nature of a problem, each other's feelings and points of view, and choose a mutually satisfying solution. Older pupils may even be able to use their greater maturity and skills of perception to help disputants identify underlying issues and unexpressed needs before generating a solution.

At primary schools pupils in Year 5 (aged 9 or 10) are often chosen to receive initial training. This is because they can learn from trained mediators in the year above

	In place	Under development	Not in place

▶▶▶ Teachers

1 Teachers welcome pupils into their classrooms.			
2 Teachers are committed to children's and young people's holistic development.			
3 Teachers teach with pace and structure while remaining flexible to individual needs.			
4 Teachers seek to understand problematic behaviour and are prepared to modify their practice if needed.			
5 Teachers use non-confrontational language in the classroom to resolve difficulties.			
6 Teachers are positive role models and adopt problem-solving approaches to conflict themselves.			

Opportunities for pupil voice/empowerment

1 Pupils have regular opportunities to contribute to school decision-making processes.			
2 Pupils are consulted about classroom and behaviour management practices.			
3 Pupils have opportunities to play a part in the running of their schools (e.g. school council).			
4 Pupils have regular opportunities to participate in co-operative as well as competitive activities.			
5 Forms of peer support complementary to mediation already exist (e.g. buddy system).			

Long-term planning and training

1 A budget or funding source has been identified to implement and sustain the service.			
2 A fully committed teacher to co-ordinate the service has been identified.			
3 Sources of external support/training have been identified and approached.			
4 Staff members are trained in behaviour management strategies consistent with the philosophy of mediation.			
5 A strategy exists to promote the service and maintain its profile.			
6 A system for further training of pupils, after the initial period of training, has been planned.			

© Mediation Matters LDA Permission to Photocopy

School readiness for peer mediation survey

	In place	Under development	Not in place

General environment/safety

1. The school is attractive, well maintained and welcoming.
2. An audit has been conducted identifying areas of the school where pupils are more vulnerable and preventative steps have been taken.
3. Rooms and corridors are spacious and systems are in place to facilitate the smooth flow of pupil traffic.
4. Pupils are able to engage in a range of freely chosen activities during break times.
5. Provision exists for pupils to keep their possessions safe.
6. The school's values and expected code of conduct are displayed clearly.
7. The school publicises its commitment to non-violent resolution of conflicts.

Policies

1. Restorative justice is a key feature of the school disciplinary system.
2. The behaviour management policy specifies a role for pupils in resolving conflict.
3. Connections exist between behaviour, health and safety and other related policies.
4. The whole school community is regularly consulted about policy development.
5. Communications with parents/carers emphasise the school's commitment to restorative justice and community cohesion.
6. Relevant policies incorporate human and children's rights legislation.
7. The procedures for dealing with violent/aggressive incidents are clearly indicated and applied consistently.
8. The procedures for challenging aggressive and demeaning language are clearly indicated and applied consistently.

Curriculum

1. Conflict resolution is a theme addressed through the curriculum (e.g. in PSHE).
2. The taught curriculum includes opportunities (such as circle time) for pupils to share and discuss issues.
3. The taught curriculum includes opportunities for pupils to develop their social and emotional skills, specifically:
   - self-awareness
   - aspects of personal safety (e.g. assertiveness)
   - empathy and respect
   - communication skills (non-verbal communication, active listening, speaking)
   - co-operation and teamwork.

There will be occasions when mediation is quiet or pupils bring made-up or inappropriate problems to mediation, but a great deal can be done by raising awareness throughout the school to ensure the service is used regularly and appropriately.

Here are some ideas to raise the profile of peer mediators and mediation as a service:

- regular demonstrations of peer mediation to other pupils;
- special assemblies;
- sharing of success stories (with clients' agreement);
- posters/displays;
- wearing caps, badges or coloured tops so that other pupils can identify mediators;
- providing form buddies – mediators who attend classes or tutor groups of younger pupils;
- induction workshops for new pupils;
- peer mediators running circle-time games;
- staff members talking about the advantages of mediation frequently and making referrals to the service as appropriate;
- peer mediator 'graduation' ceremonies to celebrate the successful completion of training.

Summary

This chapter has stated the case for peer mediation in schools and suggested a number of whole-school issues that need to be considered before a service is implemented. Research has established that mediation services can be run effectively in schools and help create more harmonious environments as a component of a broader range of initiatives. For this to happen it is necessary for schools to examine their own policies and practices, particularly how teachers manage conflict in the classroom and the way they communicate with pupils. A peer mediation service has a greater chance of success when integrated with other practices that are consistent with the underlying philosophy of mediation, when it attracts a significant level of commitment from members of staff, and when the service has a high profile.

To aid schools in evaluating whether they are ready for peer mediation, and to identify any areas in which the school needs to focus its development beforehand, a survey is provided (see pp. 24–25). The survey is divided into six sections, each drawing upon issues discussed in this chapter. Answer each question honestly and indicate whether the proposed practice is in place, under development or not in place by ticking the appropriate box. Overall, if the majority of ticks are in the 'In place' column, the school can be reassured that it is in a good position to go ahead with peer mediation training. Areas that are under development or not in place need to be addressed before, or at the very least in tandem with, peer mediation training.

such support is not always easy. However, Sharp and Thompson present evidence of effective whole-school policies resulting in tangible reductions in incidents of bullying and general aggression, sometimes within a year when there is sufficient commitment.

The work of Jerry Tyrrell, who was a significant figure in establishing mediation services in schools in Northern Ireland, is of particular interest here. In *Peer Mediation: A Process for Primary Schools* (Tyrrell 2002) he charts the stages a school needs to traverse and the problems that need to be solved in order to implement a service. As schools consider and implement peer mediation they will need to examine issues such as these:

- How will the service dovetail with whole-school policies and practices?
- How will teachers, as role models, support the service?
- How prepared are teachers to change their practice, if needed?
- How will the service relate to other school programmes (e.g. SEAL, citizenship education, pupil consultation) and behaviour management practices?
- What are the long-term plans for ownership, self-sufficiency and sustainability of the service?
- How will the service be monitored and evaluated? How will this information be used to support and develop the service?

Without due consideration of these points, peer mediation is likely to have a limited lifespan. Tyrrell's work, like mine (Sellman 2002, 2003, 2007), highlights that critical mass is not simply a sufficient number of teachers offering their vocal support for the project. If the service is to be truly successful, there needs to be general consistency between teachers' attitudes to conflict, the way they talk to pupils and the principles underpinning mediation. The implication of this is that planning a peer mediation service needs to start with adults preparing the way carefully so that mediation has the opportunity to become an integral part of school life rather than an appendage with limited utility.

Service's profile

It is essential that a peer mediation service is seen as high status and enjoys a highly visible profile. A peer mediation service can be paid no greater compliment than having teachers endorsing the language of mediation and using similar techniques as part of their own management strategies, as discussed previously. By doing so, the message is given to pupils that calm and problem-solving approaches to conflict are the most desirable and effective ones.

Clearly, those schools implementing a peer mediation service are striving to create more cohesive and harmonious environments. Peer mediators can play a significant role in the creation of this culture and their skills should be readily available to help achieve this. This also helps sustain their motivation and further develop the skills they have acquired. It is thus important that pupils can easily access the service when required (they know whom to go to, where and when).

The best way to ensure the success of peer mediation is to use the same type of language in the classroom. This helps promote the language of mediation as the way for dealing with difficult conflicts and ensures consistency of approach. By doing so, a culture of expectation is established in which mediation becomes standard, as this headteacher highlights:

> *It's not just teacher led, all the staff are trained to use the same procedures, so the lunchtime supervisors do the same thing and the children expect that if something's happened mediation will be available and they'll have an input into that mediation. They don't expect to be told off and that will be the end of everything. They expect to contribute ideas for resolution.*

An important part of developing this language is the use of a mediation script, a key component of peer mediation training (see p. 41). This constitutes a tool that can be used formally or informally by all, not just during mediation – as this teacher illustrates:

> *I think I am better now at talking with the children over a problem. I actually do use the peer mediation script when I'm dealing with two children. I don't read it out but I know the way to talk, to get one child to say something and then what to say to the other and how to make it more of a tennis match, if you like, between the two children. Whereas originally, I would have spoken to them individually with them standing in front of me ... . Instead now, I'm more, we'll hear the one side, we'll hear the other side and then we'll hear what that person's going to do and what the other person's going to do ... . And I think they've got better at that now because they immediately hear how each other is feeling.*

The use of peer mediation language like this throughout the school is perhaps the best strategy for ensuring the success of a peer mediation service, and a more democratic approach to communication and conflict resolution in general. To achieve this there needs to be considerable support from the majority of the teaching staff.

A critical mass of support for the service

> *If there's only one committed member of staff it's not enough for the work to survive. In the end they find it too difficult to maintain what they have started. There needs to be a definite commitment in senior management plus a reasonable number of other supporters. It's the concept of critical mass, it doesn't have to be everyone but a mass large enough so that the others will sway their way rather than overwhelm them with indifference and hostility.*
>
> *John Lampen, Peer mediation trainer*

Advocates of whole-school approaches (e.g. Sharp and Thompson 1994) and providers of training to schools have often used the concept of critical mass to suggest that whole-school cultural change needs the initial and ongoing support of at least a few influential members of the school community. This does not have to be every individual, but a sufficient proportion to propel and maintain change. The implementation of a peer mediation service is more likely to be successful if a school feels in control of change and is committed to the process. Gaining and maintaining

Strategies for dealing with difficult situations

Strategy	Explanation/example
Offer a choice	Gives child some control over the situation. Child is less likely to initiate point-blank refusal.
Offer some thinking time	Allows a child not to lose face. 'I shall be back to your table in two minutes and I should like to see …'
Offer a partial agreement	'Yes, you may have been talking about your work but I should like you to …'
Give a when–then direction	This is trying to avoid the negative. 'No, you cannot go out because you have not finished your work' becomes 'When you have finished your work, then you can go out.'
Use 'I' statements	Avoids blaming language. 'You're not listening' becomes 'I need you to listen so that the rest of the class can concentrate.'
Use 'You are right' statements	Engages co-operation by acknowledging the functionality of behaviour. 'You are right to show the other person you are angry. Now let me teach you another way of showing your feelings.'
Focus on the positive	Instruct pupils by telling them exactly what you would like them to do, rather than underlining what they've done wrong.
Use humour or change the topic of conversation	Deflects a child's attention from a problem and engages positive thinking.
Offer a success reminder	Reminds pupils about how they have handled a situation in the past or achieved something. This helps them identify an appropriate strategy for a difficult situation and provides necessary motivation.
Remove the audience	This creates a safe space for resolving a difficulty. A crowd may threaten a pupil with humiliation and make it difficult for them to save face. A crowd may also escalate a situation by offering inappropriate encouragement.
Convey that behaviour is a choice, ultimately with consequences	Places responsibility with the pupil. As a last resort only, communicate that everybody has to be responsible for the choices they make, which may ultimately lead to consequences.
Remember to teach behaviour	The best intervention is prevention. People make mistakes and our response should be to teach them how to avoid making the same mistakes. Punishments damage relationships and don't teach pupils what to do in the future.

Role and communication practices of teachers

Teachers have a key role to play in pupils' experiences of how to resolve conflict, so it is important that teachers are reflective practitioners and open to self-examination. Mitina (1991) highlights a range of teacher behaviours which may exacerbate experiences of interpersonal conflict at school. These include:

- typecasting of pupil behaviour and performance;
- inconsistent application of rules;
- escalation of situations owing to the immediate use of sanctions;
- setting tasks at an inappropriate level of difficulty;
- humiliating pupils in front of peers;
- giving rules which are not easy to follow;
- ignoring instances that need to be dealt with.

Such practices may undermine efforts to promote respect, empathy and peaceful approaches to conflict in schools. MacGrath (1998) also outlines a number of basic strategies associated with 'peaceful' teaching. These include a number of practical recommendations:

- ensuring that lessons are well prepared and delivered;
- setting clear boundaries for acceptable behaviour;
- being vigilant at times when conflict is more likely;
- maintaining a calm atmosphere across the school;
- rewarding good behaviour.

MacGrath advocates a number of further strategies for teachers to adopt when in a conflict situation with a pupil. These include:

- considering that they are on the same side as the pupil and empathising with them;
- viewing conflict issues as the problem, not the pupil;
- staying impartial and not becoming involved with the content of what is said, but focusing on a solution;
- being attentive to language that may escalate a conflict;
- staying calm, maintaining a relaxed and non-threatening body posture;
- being flexible about discipline.

Some teachers may be faced with quite challenging situations. In such circumstances it is important to prioritise the de-escalation of conflict. A number of strategies can be adopted to ensure that difficult situations are dealt with calmly, respectfully and positively. Some of these strategies are described in the table on page 20.

> *The aims were isolated ... and to try and do it for one hour a week when for the other twenty hours a week the regime was totally different ... teachers reacted to small groups of disruptive children by exerting their influence and control. Discipline across the school was teacher led and then they came to this one lesson where that didn't apply, where they were given responsibility for their own behaviour and they didn't cope with it very well.*

> *All the systems of reward and punishment are teacher led and mediation isn't and the two things really are going to clash. They're mutually exclusive .... There's a tradition and expectation that teachers will sort out behaviour problems and mediators are coming from a different perspective, expecting people to sort out their own problems and find their own solutions.*

Where peer mediation schemes are effective they have a great impact on roles within the school. Pupils enjoy greater responsibilities and there is a significant shift in disciplinary technique from teacher arbitration to third-party mediation. In turn, this can have an impact on the escalation of conflicts as disputes are often prevented from escalating at an early stage. One lunchtime supervisor has observed this:

> *Dinner times seem easier because lunchtime supervisors are not having to deal with the small problems, they're going to peer mediation. They are now able to spend more time with the deeper problems that peer mediation doesn't deal with.*

For many pupils peer mediation schemes are very popular because they represent a non-punitive form of discipline. They are given an opportunity to explore their problem and try and reach an agreement without the threat of sanctions, as this pupil comments:

> *If we ask the teacher, one of us might be upset because one of us might get into trouble. With peer mediators, you know you're not going to get into trouble.*

Not surprisingly, then, peer mediation schemes are better sustained in schools which have more horizontal power relations. This is characterised by collaboration between teachers, good relationships between pupils and teachers and problem-solving approaches to the management of conflict. Where this occurs, there is compatibility between the school culture and the principles of mediation. This allows the strategies used in mediation to become established as the way for dealing with difficulties concerning relationships. Hence the communication practices used by teachers are very similar to those used by mediators.

of time and effort by everyone within a school community. Initially the importance of a whole-school approach needs to be firmly established. It should incorporate the consultation of the wider community, including parents and governors. This involvement should continue into implementation.

Reviewing whole-school policy can be used to begin to bring consistency to teachers' behaviour management approaches. A peer mediation service will be more successful if there is consistency throughout the school regarding how conflict is managed and resolved. It can be very problematic if pupils go to different members of staff and get different responses. For example, if a child goes to one adult and is told to sort it out themselves, another adult arbitrates and another refers them to mediators, that child will get very mixed messages about how best to resolve a difficult conflict. Adults in schools need to hold the peer mediation service and its underpinning values in high regard. This also means that responsibility falls on them to model how best to resolve conflict and communicate positively. Behaviour management can be assertive but should not be confrontational. It is therefore essential that all staff members are trained to understand the principles of peer mediation and how they can most effectively help pupils resolve conflict.

It is helpful to consider Cohen's (1995) ideal system of conflict resolution in relation to these points. His model suggests that the majority of pupils' time should be spent conflict free because of a supportive school environment. This is an environment in which pupils communicate with each other calmly and respectfully. When conflict does arise pupils have the skills to negotiate solutions for themselves. More difficult conflicts should be mediated by peers, and only the most serious conflicts should be arbitrated by adults. When this occurs, adults should communicate calmly and fairly, and listen to both sides of any problem.

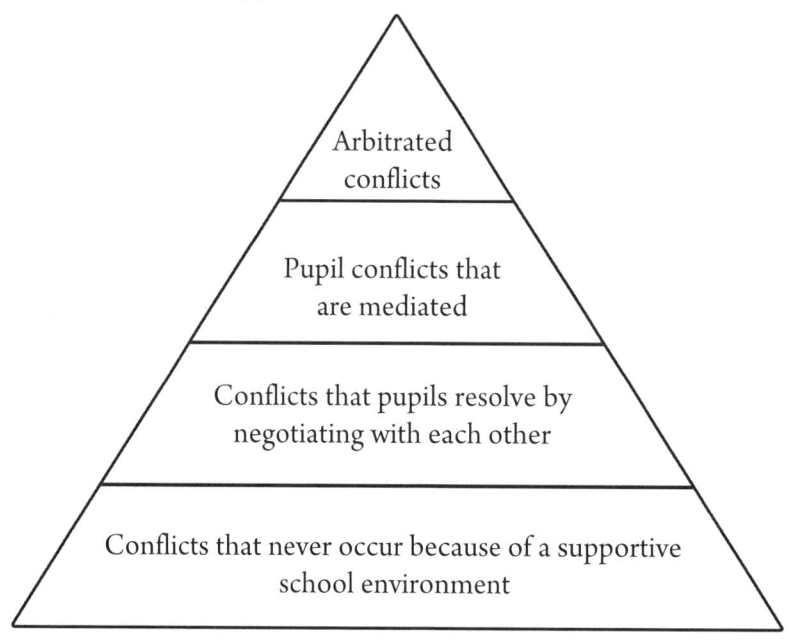

The ideal system of conflict resolution (Cohen 1995)

If Cohen's model is to be translated into practice, there needs to be agreement between how conflict is managed, the underlying principles of mediation, and the structure of power within the school. When this does not happen problems occur – as the following quotations, from senior members of staff at two schools that failed to implement peer mediation, illustrate.

Once again, training to be a peer mediator complements development in many of these areas.

Increasing importance is also being placed on the development by schools of opportunities for greater pupil involvement with the organisation of their schools (Rudduck and Fielding 2006; DfES 2007). As a result it will become important to identify and understand the processes involved in giving pupils authentic opportunities for voice and responsibility. To fulfil this aim it is necessary to differentiate between simply giving pupils opportunities to be heard or occasionally involved in school affairs, and genuine involvement in truly democratic schools. The latter is quite rare, for two reasons.

The first, in contrast to the QCA guidance previously cited, is that many schools treat pupils as citizens 'to be' rather than citizens 'here and now'. As a result issues concerning citizenship (voice, civic engagement and conflict resolution, for example) are taught as part of the curriculum, representing knowledge to be taken into the adult world. Active citizenship requires organisational changes to be made that allow pupils opportunities for democratic engagement within their schools in the present (Rudduck and Fielding 2006). When such opportunities are not made, pupil empowerment is subsequently compromised within existing structures determined by adults (Wyness 2006).

Secondly, schools often underestimate the degree and complexity of cultural change that is required for active citizenship programmes, such as peer mediation, to be meaningfully implemented. One aspect of such change is the need to reassess power relations between teachers and pupils, as discussed in the previous section. Kenway and Fitzclarence (1997) highlight the finding that interventions often focus attention on the behaviour of individuals rather than social and cultural practices. Yet such practices are crucial ingredients in whether initiatives are successful or not. In particular, Kenway and Fitzclarence propose that successful anti-violence initiatives in schools need to:

- focus on the cultural level as well as the individual;
- acknowledge the relationship between conflict resolution skills and their own organisation, policies and pedagogy;
- be prepared to give pupils some autonomy.

If peer mediators are to deploy their skills meaningfully and contribute to a wider culture of peaceful conflict resolution, each of these points is key. To meet the challenge of addressing these cultural issues it is necessary to consider the following whole-school issues:

- behaviour management structures and policy;
- the role and communication practices of teachers;
- the existence of a critical mass of support for the service;
- the service's profile.

Behaviour management structures and policy

Salisbury and Jackson (1996) emphasise that tackling violence, bullying and controlling approaches to conflict requires a whole-school approach, so that the school is seen as a consistent community that will not tolerate violence. They suggest that schools need to examine the relationship between aggressive behaviour and their own organisation, policies, discipline and teaching styles. Isolated or short-term interventions tend to have a limited impact. Sharp and Thompson (1994) recognise that an effective whole-school approach requires a huge investment

Peer mediation, citizenship and pupil voice

Peer mediation is an initiative that dovetails with many of the aims underpinning citizenship education and the Social and Emotional Aspects of Learning (SEAL) curriculum. It also represents an initiative that allows pupils greater voice and empowerment, an issue that will continue to be a feature of good practice in twenty-first-century schools. Peer mediation should not be seen as an isolated intervention, but rather as part of a wholesale cultural transition within schools towards greater pupil participation. This should be taken into consideration when planning to implement a peer mediation service.

Perhaps in recognition of the narrow curriculum introduced in 1988 and wider concerns regarding perceived political apathy and youth crime, the government required citizenship education to be taught in secondary schools by 2002. The Crick Report (QCA 1998) sets out the guidelines for citizenship education and the teaching of democracy in schools. It emphasises that the delivery of any citizenship curriculum must contain authentic experiences as well as traditional teaching methods.

> *We stress, however, that citizenship education is education for citizenship, behaving and acting as a citizen, therefore it is not just knowledge of citizenship and civic society; it also implies developing values, skills and understanding.*
>
> (QCA 1998)

Education for citizenship requires that schools need to relate whole-school issues to children's experiences of citizenship.

> *Schools need to consider to what extent their ethos, organisation and daily practices are consistent with the aim and purpose of citizenship education, and provide opportunities for pupils to develop into active citizens.*
>
> (QCA 1998)

These points are reinforced by a review of the curriculum chaired by Sir Keith Ajegbo for the Department for Education and Skills (DfES 2007), which states, 'the process of dialogue and communication must be central to pedagogical strategies for Citizenship'. 'Cooperation and conflict' is one of the eight key concepts of the citizenship curriculum cited in the Crick Report (QCA 1998), and conflict resolution is an integral theme. Clearly, training in conflict resolution and peer mediation represents a vehicle for delivering these elements and helping develop a co-operative and democratic school.

In the light of evidence emphasising the centrality of emotion to the learning process and broader mental well-being, the DfES introduced the SEAL curriculum for schools (DfES 2005). It includes assemblies, activities and lessons on five key areas:

- self-awareness
- managing feelings
- empathy
- motivation
- social skills.

cohesive school culture. On the other hand, it is also clear that this happens only when services are implemented carefully and when there is synergy between the philosophy of mediation and the existing or developing culture in the school.

Research about peer mediation has been carried out in both the US and the UK. Garcia et al. (2006) have conducted a systematic review of conflict resolution and peer mediation programmes in schools. Their review included ten studies from Australia, Canada and the US which met tight selection criteria, and indicated long-lasting benefits for pupils who are taught conflict resolution skills. Such programmes are particularly effective in developing pupils' understanding of conflict and broadening the range of resolution strategies they can recall.

One of the studies from which favourable findings emerged (Johnson and Johnson 1996) concluded that:

- pupils trained as peer mediators learn and retain conflict resolution skills;
- the successful implementation of peer mediation services results in a reduction in the number of interpupil conflicts referred to teachers for arbitration;
- 85–95 per cent of conflicts mediated by peers result in lasting and stable agreements.

However, many of the studies identified in the review (Garcia et al. 2006) were based on curriculum projects. In these studies pupils' knowledge of conflict resolution greatly increased but the skills acquired weren't always transferred into real-life situations. This is a common problem, familiar to teachers whatever is being taught. Studies in which peer mediation was fully implemented, and thus provided pupils with experiential learning opportunities, are under-represented.

Other studies approach the evaluation of interventions such as peer mediation using 'softer' approaches, including case studies. These approaches do not necessarily churn out great quantities of scientifically robust and generalisable data, yet they yield potentially more relevant accounts of processes in schools which school leaders and teachers may find more useful. One advantage of more intensive and detailed studies is their ability to comment in depth about what can go wrong, as well as on what can go right.

The notion of synergy between the school ethos and the principles underlying peer mediation is an important finding of research by Jerry Tyrrell (2002). He argues that the principles of peer mediation give greater authority to pupils and this contrasts with the hierarchical relationships common to many schools. Some teachers and lunchtime supervisors in his and similar studies (Griffith 1996; Knight and Sked 1998) found it difficult to hand over some of this authority to pupils.

In my research (Sellman 2003) a number of issues were identified that were characteristic of peer mediation services being successfully implemented and sustained long term. These were:

- schools were committed to pupil empowerment;
- peer mediators were trained at a time when they were able to undertake their role for at least twelve months and then assisted in cycles of training for future mediators;
- behaviour management policies were consistent with peer mediation;
- teachers used and modelled positive language when resolving conflict;
- services were given a high profile (see p. 23 for a list of ways to raise the profile of the service).

2 Case for peer mediation and whole-school issues to consider

This chapter will begin by stating the case, based on research evidence, for peer mediation. It will demonstrate that peer mediation works. Once a peer mediation service has been set up, pupils will have learned a greater range of ways to resolve conflict and teachers can expect to spend less time arbitrating conflicts because pupils are able to support each other. Peer mediation also gives young people authentic responsibilities, which helps fulfil the aims of a broader citizenship education to provide pupils with opportunities for voice and a role in the governance of their schools. If these significant dividends are to materialise, the school needs to invest heavily in the underlying philosophy of mediation.

The remainder of the chapter will discuss a number of critical issues that should be evaluated and considered realistically before a service can be implemented. These include the need for pupils to be given genuine and meaningful opportunities for voice and empowerment, which may mean that staff members should change the way they view authority and talk about conflict. This is in addition to the necessary investment of teacher time, training, money and resources to support and maintain the service fully.

The chapter will conclude with a survey that schools can use to identify whether they are ready to implement a peer mediation service, and the areas they need to address beforehand if they are not (see pp. 24–25). Schools should not be reluctant to undertake such an exercise. Preparatory work at this stage will mean a peer mediation service is much more likely to succeed initially and then last. Most importantly, as a component of a carefully prepared school development plan, a peer mediation service can help bring about a sustainable and positive cultural change in schools.

Research evidence for peer mediation

The literature on conflict has tended to concentrate upon its destructive aspects and either its elimination or avoidance, yet conflict can promote learning and development when managed effectively. Many educationalists advocate that children are taught how to harness the potentially constructive aspects of conflict in order to develop their own skills, improve relationships and learn how to resolve opposing stances peacefully (Cohen 1995).

The message from research studies evaluating peer mediation services is quite clear. On the one hand, they yield exciting and encouraging results, showing that peer mediation services can be very effective in at least two ways. They provide pupils with valuable opportunities to develop communicational and conflict resolution skills, and they contribute to a more harmonious and

Under the guidance of peer mediators, disputants follow a process in which pupils:

- introduce themselves;
- agree to the ground rules;
- define the problem in turn and in their own words;
- explore each other's wants, needs and feelings;
- generate potential solutions;
- agree a solution.

In contrast to mediators, arbitrators exercise much greater power and authority in determining both process and outcome. They may listen to different accounts of the conflict, but ultimately they assume responsibility for deciding upon and imposing an outcome. In schools a lot of teacher time can be spent in this role.

Summary

This chapter has provided a basic overview of the characteristics of conflict and ways of resolving it. The process of peer mediation as a form of conflict resolution has been outlined, as well as the history of such services in schools. It is now time to turn our attention to whole-school issues so that the decision to implement a peer mediation service can be made with a full and realistic understanding of the requirements and demands this will place on school structures, personnel and resources.

Process of peer mediation

The role of the third party varies greatly between arbitration and mediation. Peer mediation offers pupils experiencing a conflict the opportunity to reach a mutually satisfying outcome facilitated by neutral third parties from amongst their peers. Peer mediators are impartial; they insist only that certain ground rules are kept.

These rules typically include:

- using each other's names;
- listening to each other without interrupting;
- not blaming the other person;
- keeping the contents of the meeting private;
- genuinely wanting to solve the problem.

Each of these rules is important. As mediation is a voluntary process with a significant role for disputants, they both must want genuinely to solve the problem for the process to be successful. Those who cannot keep the rules and who thus sabotage the process or who visibly do not want mediation (e.g. their back is turned, or they are abusive) are not yet ready to use mediation, and the process should either be halted or not started. As a mark of respect and to ensure a smooth process, disputants and mediators should refer to each other by name, and all should refrain from judging the situation and attaching blame. The emphasis of the process is on identifying what can be done in the future to address what has happened in the past.

A large proportion of peer mediation training is dedicated to communication skills and active listening. This involves listening to what someone has to say and saying it back to them as accurately as possible once they have finished. During this process, disputants have the opportunity to express their version of events and their associated feelings. As it is often the emotional needs of a situation that need resolving (such as feeling left out) rather than the behavioural aspects of a conflict (such as an argument about missing a turn in a game), the formal mediation process may be the first opportunity disputants have to hear about the other's feelings. Addressing issues concerning feelings often proves to be the catalyst for achieving a resolution.

Mediators stay impartial throughout this process. They remind disputants of the rules but generally they are there to facilitate a process in which the pupils decide upon an agreement to resolve their problem from a range of alternatives. With very young children, mediators can be trained to offer some guidance and even some appropriate alternatives for them to choose from. Mature and experienced mediators working with older pupils can use their skills to help disputants identify some of the more subtle and complex nuances underpinning their conflict. It is important that disputants can trust the mediators – that they will stay impartial, manage the process competently and keep their confidence. Mediators need to explain clearly but delicately to disputants what can and cannot be kept confidential. To safeguard children and young people it should be made clear that issues of a criminal nature and those that raise child protection issues cannot be discussed without being referred to someone with appropriate authority. Mediators should also explain that they will make it absolutely clear to the disputants if such an issue arises and what will happen if further material is disclosed.

Arbitration by adults may sometimes be problematic also as they frequently don't have sufficient time to resolve the conflict in a manner acceptable to both (or all) pupils involved. Hence the conflict may remain unresolved or resolved via a quick fix, which may not address the underlying issues. As previously stated, the subjects of pupils' conflicts may appear trivial to teachers, but the underlying feelings can be genuinely upsetting for the disputants. If these are not satisfactorily resolved harmony and learning in the classroom may be seriously affected.

Peer mediation offers a number of advantages to the resolution of difficult conflicts. These are:

- pupils are trained in the key skills needed for settling their own disputes;
- mediators are available to assist other pupils experiencing difficult conflicts;
- the voluntary nature of peer mediation allows disputants risk-free opportunities to solve their problems;
- mediation can take place soon after an incident and does not need to be rushed;
- mediation often results in common-sense solutions.

History of peer mediation

Conflict resolution programmes in schools, including peer mediation, first emerged in American schools in the early 1970s (Tyrrell and Farrell 1995). This was preceded by a growing interest in the subject of conflict resolution as an academic discipline following the Second World War and a peace movement that grew in momentum during the 1960s (Cohen 1995; Stacey, Robinson and Cremin 1997). Isenhart and Spangle (2000) recall how the Quakers were instrumental in implementing such programmes and describe the Children's Project for Friends as the first to teach principles of non-violence in New York schools. Isenhart and Spangle estimated that there were over 6,000 conflict resolution programmes in schools in the United States at the approach of the millennium.

During the late 1980s and the 1990s the use of peer mediation spread to other parts of the world. It was already prevalent in North America and Australasia and becoming more common in Europe. In the UK, through the Quakers once more, the Education for Mutual Understanding project in Northern Ireland, the West Midlands Quaker Peace Education Project and the Kingston Friends Workshop Group were among the first to introduce peer mediation from the United States into UK schools (Tyrrell and Farrell 1995). Conflict resolution now forms a key element of citizenship education in schools and, in the light of recent policy developments, I expect the number of peer mediation services in UK schools to continue to grow.

Peer mediation as a specific form of conflict resolution

As mediation and arbitration involve third parties, they are approaches usually reserved for conflicts that are difficult to resolve. As a conflict moves from independent negotiation (how most conflicts are normally resolved) to mediation to arbitration, the process becomes increasingly formal, with greater authority assigned to a third party. The power is more balanced in mediation as mediators merely facilitate the process, putting the onus on disputants to generate their own solutions to their conflict. In arbitration, the third party has the power to adjudicate the conflict and determine any subsequent action to be taken.

The differences between mediation and arbitration are summarised in the following table.

Differences between mediation and arbitration

Mediation	Arbitration
Power is disputant centred	Power is arbitrator centred
Non-judgemental third party	Judgemental third party
Non-punitive	Punitive
Future-orientated	Focused on the past
Win–win agreement	Win–lose decision
Voluntary	Participation often mandatory
Dispute defined and explored by the disputants	Dispute defined by the arbitrator
Confidential (unless serious issues disclosed)	Confidentiality often not raised as an issue

Adapted from Cohen 1995

Arbitration is generally located within a **punitive** disciplinary framework, common in hierarchical organisations. Arbitration attempts to allocate blame for the conflict and assign a punishment. This is a typical feature of traditional approaches to discipline in schools: fixed, abstract and corrective. In contrast, mediation is located within a **restorative** disciplinary framework which is often used in situations where relationships are identified as interdependent. The emphasis of this approach to conflict resolution is on healing any damage done to the relationship between the parties and ensuring a positive relationship in the future. Rather than administering punishment, the role of the mediator is to facilitate this process and encourage disputants to generate their own solutions to the problem. This approach to discipline may be described as flexible, contextual and reparative.

Most pupils in schools only have a choice between two possibilities for resolving their conflicts: negotiation (resolving the conflict by themselves) or arbitration (by adults on their behalf). Pupils choosing to negotiate their own conflicts sometimes lack the knowledge and skills to do this and either avoid resolving the conflict or resolve it inappropriately, with violence or aggression.

Strategies for resolving conflict

There are lots of different ways to resolve conflicts. The specific approach to resolving conflict adopted may vary according to how much the disputants value the people they are in conflict with and the degree of importance assigned to the issues underpinning the conflict, as represented in the grid below.

Approaches to resolving conflict

		Value for relationships	
		High	**Low**
Value for conflict	**High**	Compromise/Collaboration (win–win)	Controlling (win–lose)
	Low	Accommodation (yield–win)	Avoidance (lose–lose)

Adapted from an original model by Blake and Mouton 1964

A conflict outcome may be described in terms of winners and losers. For example, a controlling approach to conflict, adopted when the matter under dispute is valued more highly than the relationship with the disputant, usually results in one winner and a loser (a win–lose outcome). Violent resolutions to conflict are not desirable because they involve a winner and a loser. In other situations, those involved in conflict may yield to another's wishes because they care more about the relationship than the conflict. When neither the relationship nor issues relating to the conflict are valued very highly, the conflict tends to be avoided altogether. Alternatively, a collaborative approach usually results in a win–win outcome. This is advantageous as both parties are happy and are therefore more likely to maintain any agreement made to resolve the conflict. As a result, the conflict is likely to be resolved in a lasting manner. The implications of trying to facilitate as many win–win outcomes as possible in schools are threefold:

- Pupils need to be able to identify clearly what their needs and goals are.
- These need to be balanced by a concern for the needs and goals of others.
- Relationships between members of the school community need to be cohesive and respectful.

The last point above is very important. It stresses the centrality of relationships at the core of peaceful and mutually satisfying conflict resolution. An understanding of relationships, and skills in empathy, respect and communication, need to inform the training process. Perhaps even more importantly, these attitudes and skills need to be modelled by staff members and school structures.

Clearly, some conflicts are more difficult to resolve independently than others and may benefit from the help of a third party. There are two prominent approaches to resolving such difficult conflicts. These are arbitration and mediation, and the role of third parties in each approach differs fundamentally. Both approaches are discussed in the next section.

Escalation and de-escalation (and a role for third parties)

Conflicts vary in intensity from a brief exchange of angry remarks to more heated arguments that may go on for days. Some interpersonal conflicts may involve just two disputants, whereas others may become more complicated and involve several others, including teachers. Similarly, physical conflicts may be over as quickly as they began or be protracted over some time. The level of violence may vary greatly and in some cases be very serious.

Bystanders have an influential role to play regarding the escalation or de-escalation of conflicts.

Actions that escalate conflicts include:

- watching conflict as if it's entertainment;
- cheering and encouraging;
- adding fuel to the issues being disputed (gossiping, spreading rumours and so on);
- taking a side and joining in;
- discouraging others from de-escalating.

Actions that de-escalate conflicts include:

- getting help;
- intervening (when safe to do so) or asking disputants to stop;
- reassuring disputants and offering alternatives;
- using a sense of humour or alternative strategies to distract the disputants;
- offering mediation.

The choices that bystanders make in conflict will have a significant impact on the experience of conflict and whether the outcomes are constructive or destructive.

Constructive outcomes are those when:

- opportunities for learning are presented;
- communication skills are developed;
- important issues are opened up or problems are highlighted;
- trust is developed;
- anxiety, suspicion and stress are relieved.

Destructive outcomes are those when:

- issues are left unresolved or not resolved satisfactorily;
- fear and anxiety are created;
- confidence and self-esteem are lowered;
- energy is diverted from more important issues;
- creativity is suppressed;
- attitudes become entrenched;
- aggressive or violent behaviour occurs, which may lead to injury to oneself or others.

Whether conflict is a constructive or destructive experience depends upon the strategies chosen by disputants and other parties.

It is helpful to view conflict not as a one-off incident, such as a fight or an argument (a behavioural emphasis), but as a culmination of a series of events underpinned by an individual's genuine needs and wishes (a functional emphasis). People rarely argue or fight for the sake of it. When the issues are later identified and analysed, it is clear that people normally act in ways to meet their own psychological and functional goals. These may include the need to protect themselves, those close to them or what they have; or the need for greater attention, affection, power or occasionally revenge for previous experiences.

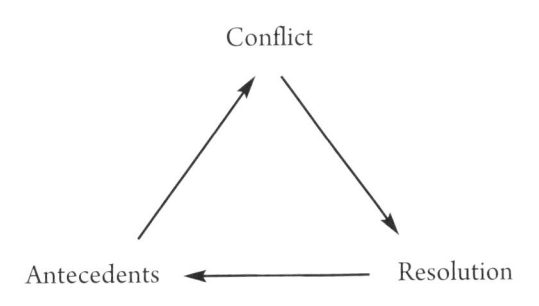

```
              Conflict
              /\
             /  \
            /    \
           /      ↘
Antecedents ←———— Resolution
```

Conflict resolution theorists identify stages, or cycles, common to most conflicts: antecedents (prior experiences), experience of conflict and an aftermath (a resolution), which in turn will become the antecedents of future conflicts. Pupils who train to become peer mediators will need to understand this, and it should form part of their training.

It is wise not to assume that all school contexts are the same. School communities and the organisation of schools themselves vary enormously. However, pupils and teachers at all schools share the same space and have to learn to co-exist peacefully. It is well worth thinking about how the context of a school affects people's experiences of conflict. Schools where there are pro-educational attitudes, a broad curriculum, positive role models, democratic processes, opportunities for student voice and co-operative climates are much more likely to encourage positive approaches to conflict. These important points will be considered in the next chapter.

Problematic issues under dispute

Interpersonal conflicts involve two or more sides taking mutually exclusive stances, whether physical or not, over an issue perceived to be problematic. Sometimes these issues, such as an argument over an object or friendship matter, may seem quite trivial to teachers, but they are very real to those concerned. This is often because the trivial matter under conflict is underpinned by emotional needs and histories, as previously discussed, and hence the distress experienced is genuine.

Children will inevitably experience a great deal of conflict during their school career and this will almost certainly continue into later life. However, conflict is not necessarily problematic; in fact it is an essential component of learning and development. It is how conflict is managed that should concern parents, carers, teachers and other professionals. Many children experience conflict on a daily basis but resolve their difficulties quickly and non-violently. However, children will also experience conflicts which they need help to resolve, such as arguments and friendship difficulties, as well as less frequent incidents of verbal abuse, unpleasant text messages or e-mails, or even violence.

1 What is peer mediation?

Before a peer mediation service can be implemented in a school it is essential to understand fully what such a service involves and the demands it will place on a school. This is best built upon a basic understanding of conflict resolution theory. This chapter will provide an overview of different ways of resolving conflict and highlight peer mediation as a specific form of conflict resolution. The chapter will also include sections on the history of peer mediation in schools and its unique process.

Characteristics of conflict

The *Oxford English Dictionary* defines 'conflict' as a fight, struggle or clash. The word is derived from the Latin word *confligere*, meaning 'to strike together'. On one hand, a conflict can be a struggle or clash between opposing beliefs and ideas; on the other hand, conflict can represent an actual physical clash. This means that conflict can be experienced inside someone's mind (e.g. not knowing what to do in a difficult situation) or enacted between two or more people's minds (e.g. alternative ideas when arguing about how to do something). Sometimes a conflict can become physical, such as when two or more people push each other, snatch things from one another or exchange kicks and punches. Conflicts brought to peer mediation are likely to include disagreements about friendships, games and objects, name-calling and perhaps even bullying. These conflicts concern the situations pupils face every day and their interactions with each other. Given the nature of these conflicts and the scope of this book, this brief overview of conflict resolution theory will focus upon interpersonal conflicts in schools. Examples of this type of conflict are shown in the conflict cartoons on page 40.

Whereas the nature of conflict is highly dependent on the situation in which it arises, there are a number of characteristics that all conflicts have in common. These include a history and context, problematic issues under dispute, factors that may escalate or de-escalate the conflict (including a role for third parties), different strategies that each party may adopt, and ultimately a resolution which may be either constructive or destructive.

History and context

All conflicts have a history: a set of events and relationships that preceded the situation that is currently affected by the conflict. In schools such 'history' may include the friendships and allies that have been forged and broken in the past, the identities people have that are at stake or the outcomes of previous conflicts. These experiences will also correlate with a range of emotions that different people will bring to a conflict situation. Feelings of fear, excitement or revenge, previous successes and failures, and cultural expectations will all contribute to the positions people will adopt in conflict.

Introduction

The aim of this book is to provide an introductory yet comprehensive guide to implementing a peer mediation service in your school. It will provide an overview of the whole process: from deciding whether peer mediation is appropriate for your school to setting up a service and evaluating its impact. Peer mediation is a strategy for giving pupils ownership of the conflict resolution process, and it relates to aspects of the curriculum, such as learning objectives within citizenship and PSHE, and to whole-school issues, such as behaviour management and anti-bullying. In providing this outline I shall draw upon my experience as both a practitioner and a researcher. That includes several years developing peer mediation in schools while working for the West Midlands Quaker Peace Education Project and also my PhD research. These experiences allow me to comment on what can go wrong as well as on what can go right.

This book is aimed at headteachers and senior teachers considering peer mediation; teachers with an existing responsibility for co-ordinating a peer mediation service and those thinking about implementing a new service; teachers wishing to introduce conflict resolution or peer mediation training within PSHE, citizenship or literacy; practitioners of peer mediation training and specialists interested in behaviour in schools.

A peer mediation service is a system within which pupils who are trained in mediation help other children to resolve conflicts successfully. When implemented meaningfully as part of a broader commitment to pupil empowerment and voice, peer mediation has radical implications for how relationships, communication and conflict are managed in a school. Peer mediation requires a significant commitment of time and resources and the ability of staff members to trust pupils with an active role in their school. However, it is an investment worth making as it can be part of a process that brings greater harmony and significant life-enhancing learning for all involved.

The broad aims of peer mediation include to:

- develop pupils' (and staff members') understanding of relationships, communication and conflicts;
- develop pupils' (and staff members') conflict resolution skills;
- increase the range of opportunities pupils in conflict have to choose from;
- involve pupils in the management of their schools and thus develop their identity as active citizens;
- help build a calm, cohesive and emotionally literate school community.

This book is organised into three parts to guide the reader through the process of implementing a peer mediation service. Part I will introduce conflict resolution and peer mediation, and will discuss a number of whole-school issues to consider before deciding whether to introduce a service in your school. Part II provides an overview of the training process and will discuss a number of issues regarding the implementation of a service. This includes an example of a training programme which can be used as a framework to be adapted for use in schools. Part III discusses issues concerning the monitoring and evaluation of peer mediation services and how to ensure their sustainability. A case study of a school that has successfully implemented and sustained a peer mediation service concludes the book.

Contents

Introduction 4

Part I: Before implementing peer mediation 5

1 What is peer mediation? 5
  – Characteristics of conflict 5
  – Strategies for resolving conflict 8
  – Peer mediation as a specific form of conflict resolution 9
  – History of peer mediation 10
  – Process of peer mediation 11

2 Case for peer mediation and whole-school issues to consider 13
  – Research evidence for peer mediation 13
  – Peer mediation, citizenship and pupil voice 15
  – Behaviour management structures and policy 16
  – Role and communication practices of teachers 19
  – A critical mass of support for the service 21
  – Service's profile 22
  – School readiness for peer mediation survey 24

Part II: Implementing peer mediation 26

3 Peer mediation training 26
  – Starting points 26
  – Training as a process 27
  – Key skills 28
  – Sample scheme of work 29

4 Implementing a peer mediation service 41
  – Further training 41
  – Peer mediation scripts 41
  – Example of a training programme 45
  – Training for other key people 52
  – Managing the early stages 52
  – What ifs 52

Part III: After implementing peer mediation 55

5 Monitoring and evaluating peer mediation 55
  – On what terms should peer mediation be evaluated? 55
  – Approaches to evaluation 57

6 Sustaining peer mediation 60
  – Case study – Dovecote Primary School 60
  – Key themes 62

References 64